SCHOOL LIBRARY SERVICE

DISCOVERING SACRED TEXTS

Series editor:
W. Owen Cole

Hindu
Scriptures

V.P. (Hemant) Kanitkar

HEINEMANN

Heinemann Library
an imprint of Heinemann Publishers (Oxford) Ltd
Halley Court, Jordan Hill, Oxford OX2 8EJ

OXFORD LONDON EDINBURGH
MADRID ATHENS BOLOGNA PARIS
MELBOURNE SYDNEY AUCKLAND SINGAPORE
TOKYO IBADAN NAIROBI HARARE
GABORONE PORTSMOUTH NH (USA)

© V. P. (Hemant) Kanitkar 1994

First published 1994

**A catalogue record for this book is
available from the British Library**

ISBN 0 431 07373 2
98 97 96 95 94
10 9 8 7 6 5 4 3 2 1

Designed and produced by Visual Image,Street
Cover design by Philip Parkhouse, Abingdon
Produced by Mandarin Offset
Printed and bound in Hong Kong

Introduction to the series

The purpose of these books is to show what the scriptures of the six religions in the series are, to tell the story of how they grew into their present form, and to give some idea of how they are used and what they mean to believers. It is hoped that readers will be able to appreciate how important the sacred texts are to those who base their lives on them and use them to develop their faith as well as their knowledge. For this reason, members of the six major religions found in Britain today have been asked to write these books.

W. Owen Cole (Series Editor)

Acknowledgements

The author wishes to thank Owen Cole for his encouragement, suggestions and guidance; Ramesh Dogra and Stephanie Ramamurthy of the School of Oriental and African Studies, University of London, for their invaluable help in locating Hindu scripture material; his wife, Dr Helen A. Kanitkar for her unfailing support and for checking the proofs; Raksha Thaker for providing transliteration of the Gayatri verse in Gujarati script; and Barbara Nelson-Smith for preparing the final typescript.

The Publishers would like to thank the following for permission to reproduce photographs: Circa Photo Library p.11; Bruce Coleman Ltd p.8; Format Partners p.37; Sally and Richard Greenhill pp.38, 44; The Hutchison Library p.36; Hemant Kanitkar p.13, 34; Ann and Bury Peerless pp.5, 9, 10, 12, 14, 24, 25, 26, 27, 28, 30, 32, 33, 46, 47; Vrindaban Research Institute pp.6, 16, 18, 43; Yeshwant Mali p.22.

The Publishers would like to thank the Vrindaban Research Institute (scripture) and W. Owen Cole (worshippers) for the cover photographs.

The Publishers would like to thank the following for permission to reproduce copyright material: Columbia University Press, *Sources of Indian Tradition*, edited by William T. deBary, 1958, for the boxed quotations on pp. 17, 21, 25, 31, 41, 43; Princeton University Press, *A Sourcebook for Indian Philosophy*, edited by S. Radhakrishnan and C.A. Moore, 1973, for the boxed quotations on pp. 5, 29, 45; Prinit Press, *An Indian Peasant Mystic*, edited by J. S. Hoyland, for 'The Sense of Sin' on p. 9; The Seabury Press, *The Smokeless Fire*, edited by Catherine Hughes, 1974, for the boxed quotations on pp 7, 15, 19. All other quotations from scriptures translated by the Author.

The Publishers have made every effort to trace copyright holders. However, if any material has been incorrectly acknowledged, we would be pleased to correct this at the earliest opportunity.

Contents

1 Hinduism: the One and the Many

This unit is about the many forms of Hinduism which are found in India.

If you look at the trees in a park, flowers in a shop, birds in a garden or animals in a zoo, you will see their wide variety. If you look at any group of people you will notice similarities and differences among them. This can be true of a crowd at a football match or the school sports day; your class; even your family.

Looked at one way, they are all different. No two people have the same fingerprints or DNA structure. Even twins, who may look alike, can have many differences. One may be vegetarian and another may eat meat, for example, or they may have different interests. Of course, there are things which even the most different-looking people have in common. All human beings walk erect, unlike other animals. All make things, not only as tools, as some animals do, but for enjoyment, e.g. musical instruments.

India is a large country almost the size of Europe. Its people speak many languages and follow a variety of religions. Most of them are Hindus who practise their faith in different ways. This book is about the many sacred texts which they share, but we must begin with some Hindu beliefs about God, because the scriptures are about God and Hindus believe that God gave them to humankind, to help men and women know God and to live happy lives.

Brahman the One God

God is One but people understand God in many ways. The One God which Hindus worship is called **Brahman**. It is a spirit without any form. To make it more meaningful to ordinary people, this spirit is often given a form which Hindus call a **murti** or **rupa**. The three most important appearances of Brahman are as the Creator (Brahma), the Preserver (Vishnu) and the Destroyer (Shiva), with their wives, Saraswati, Lakshmi and Parvati (the Mother Goddess, sometimes called Shakti). Today, Vishnu,

Shiva and Shakti are widely worshipped by Hindus. Two other appearances of Brahman are Ganesha and Hanuman.

Hindus have many sacred books written in different languages using different scripts. Most Indian languages are written from left to right.

The Gayatri verse

> 'We focus our minds on the perfect splendour of the Sun God, who sustains the Earth, the Interspace and the Heavens. May the Sun God inspire our thoughts.'

The Gayatri verse from the **Rig-Veda**, the oldest Hindu scripture, is used by many Hindus in morning worship.

In the very distant past the sacred teachings of Hinduism were composed in ancient **Sanskrit**. They were not written down because they were considered very sacred. They were passed on from teacher to pupil by word of mouth for many centuries. The texts were preserved through the **oral tradition** before they were written down some 3000 years after they were originally composed. 'Hearing' the sacred words is still very important to many Hindus even though their sacred books are now available in printed form.

The Gayatri verse in Sanskrit and Gujarati scripts.

ॐ भूर्भुवः स्वः । ॐ तत्सवितुर्वरेण्यं भर्गो देवस्य धीमहि । धियो यो नः प्रचोदयात्

ॐ ભૂર્ભુવ: સ્વ: તત્સવિતુર્વરેણ્યં ભર્ગો દેવસ્ય ધીમહિ ધિયોન: પ્રચોદયાત્

A priest reading a sacred book in a Hindu temple. The other people are listening to him; they have come to the temple after bathing in the morning to listen to the sacred words, and to express their devotion to God. The priest explains the Sanskrit text in a regional language such as Hindi, Bengali or Gujarati.

NEW WORDS

Brahman the Supreme Spirit of Hinduism

Gayatri verse the widely used prayer from the Rig-Veda, praising the Sun God

Murti or rupa an image of a god or goddess used in worship. It can be human, animal, plant or bird, or a combination of these

Oral tradition the way early Hindus passed on sacred texts by word of mouth to the next generation

Rig-Veda the oldest Hindu scripture

Sanskrit an ancient language of India. Many Hindu scriptures are written in Sanskrit

To Agni [the god of fire]
'I praise Agni, the Purohita [priest], the divine ministrant of the sacrifice, the Hotr priest, the greatest bestower of treasures.'
Agni, worthy to be praised by the ancient sages and by the present ones – may he conduct the gods hither.   (Rig-Veda: I.1.1–2)

To Varuna
'What sin we have ever committed against a relation, O Varuna, against a friend or companion at any time, a brother, a neighbour, or a stranger, that, O Varuna, take from us.
If like gamblers at play we have cheated, whether in truth or without knowing, all that take from us, O God. So may we be dear to thee, O Varuna.'   (Rig-Veda v.85)

To Visvedevas [All gods]
'To what is one, sages give many a title: they call it Agni, Yama (King of the Departed), Matarisvan.'   (Rig-Veda: I.164.46)

2 The many scriptures of Hinduism

This unit tells you about the variety of Hindu scriptures and how they developed over many centuries.

The earliest scriptures, the Vedas, were composed by the Aryans, who began to settle in north-west India in about 1500BCE. The Vedas, or Vedic texts, praise the One God under different names such as Indra, Vishnu, Rudra, Prajapati and Agni, and contain **mantras** which are used in many ceremonies like the sacred thread (see Unit 5) and marriage. Goddesses such as Prithivi (Earth) and Ushas (Dawn) have a small role in the Vedas. Today Vishnu, Rudra and Prajapati are worshipped as Vishnu, Shiva and Brahma, and the goddesses have an important role in modern Hindu worship.

There are four Vedas. Each one contains

- hymns of praise
- instructions for fire rituals
- prayers used in worship and meditation
- discussions between teachers and pupils.

These scriptures were composed over a long period of time and preserved through oral tradition.

After the Vedas had been composed, more scriptures were created, setting down the rules for religious rituals which people performed in their own homes. These were followed by the 'law books', which give rules for religious and social behaviour. Then there were two very long poems (epics), which told the stories of earlier heroes. The epics repeated many philosophical and moral ideas from the later Vedic texts. The most important scripture of modern Hinduism, the Bhagavad-Gita, was composed at the same time as the epics.

The scriptures of modern Hinduism are called the **Puranas**. These mainly deal with the worship of Brahma, Vishnu, Shiva and the Mother Goddess. They were written over a period of about 1000 years. There are eighteen important Puranas.

Many scriptures were composed by different authors at different historical times. Ideas about God, worship and 'right and wrong' from the earlier texts were repeated in

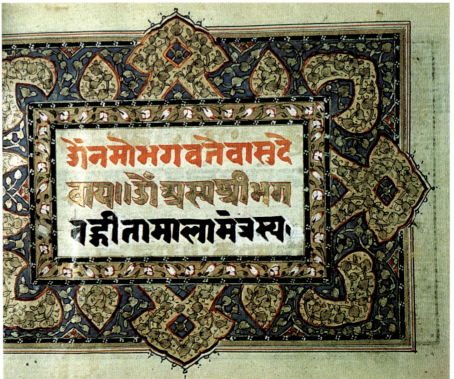

A page from a Sanskrit text showing the decorative border and clear script.

Important sacred texts	
Probable date	**Name of text**
1200–1000BCE	The Rig-Veda, the Sama-Veda, the Yajur-Veda and the Atharva-Veda. The first part of each Veda contains hymns praising God under different names.
800–500BCE	The Brahmanas, giving rules for fire rituals.
400–200BCE	The Aranyakas, containing prayers for worship meditation.
400–200BCE	The Upanishads, containing discussions of philosophy between teachers and pupils.
500–100BCE	The Sutras, short sayings or verses based on the Vedas.
c. 200BCE	Grihya Sutras, giving mantras and rules for rituals carried out at home.
200BCE	**Yoga** Sutras by Patanjali.
200BCE–200CE	Dharmashastras, the 'law books'. The law book of Manu deals with religious rituals, law, customs and politics, and puts people into groups based on their natural talents.
100BCE–100CE	The Ramayana by Valmiki, telling the story of Prince Rama.
300BCE–300CE	The Mahabharata, telling the story of the Kauravas and Pandavas.
c. 250CE	The Bhagavad-Gita, in the Mahabharata.
500–1500CE	The Puranas. The Bhagavata Purana, composed in about 900CE, is widely read. The Brahma Purana gives procedures for temple worship.
1527–1623CE	Tulsidas - Rama Charita Manasa, in Hindi.
c. 1400CE	The Vedas were first written down.
c. 1480CE	Mirabai – devotional songs in Hindi.
1440–1518CE	Kabir – devotional songs in Hindi.

later scriptures, continuing the religious tradition.

Early scriptures were in Vedic and Sanskrit languages, but from about the seventh century CE, they were brought to the ordinary people through writings in regional Indian languages. So not all the Hindu sacred texts are in Sanskrit. The scriptures deal with all aspects of Hindu belief and practice.

NEW WORDS

Mantra a sacred phrase from scriptures

Puranas ancient texts containing Hindu mythology

Yoga a system of philosophy which combines control of the mind and physical exercises to achieve freedom of the soul. It is also used simply to mean meditation

'May the breezes be sweet; may the rivers flow with sweet waters; may the herbs give us sweet (soothing) fluids; may the night and dawn be sweet...may the plants [and fruit] provide sweet juices; may the sun make us healthy; and may our cattle give us naturally sweet milk.'
(Yajur-veda Vajasaneyi-Samhita – 13.27)

'Even as a mirror stained by dust
Shines brilliantly when it has been cleansed,
so the embodied one, on seeing the nature of the Soul
Becomes one with God, his end attained, from sorrow freed....
By knowing God one is released from all earthly chains!'   (Svetasvatara Upanishad)

3 How a Hindu's day begins

This unit shows how bathing, worship of the sun and meditation are important to many Hindus.

Bathing

Wherever they live, most Hindus begin the day by bathing to clean their bodies and refresh their spirits. Some are lucky enough to be able to bathe in a sacred river, but most people bathe at home. While bathing, they may chant the name of their family god or goddess, or a mantra – a sacred phrase – containing the name Ganga (a river goddess).

Some may chant a verse from the Puranas, praising holy rivers, in order to purify their spirits. Two commonly used verses are:

> 'Honoured Goddesses of the holy rivers Ganga, Yamuna, Godavari, Saraswati, Narmada, Sindhu and Kaveri, purify this water by your divine presence.'

> 'Protect me by your compassion, Mother Ganga, and wash away all my sins.'

Offering worship to the sun

This form of worship is explained in an ancient sacred text called the *Taittiriya Aranyaka*, which is a part of the Veda. The text recommends that:

> 'Water blessed by the chanting of the Gayatri verse be offered to the sun every day.'

Many Hindus still perform this worship as part of their daily routine. The key mantra from the *Taittiriya Aranyaka* is 'Asau Adityo Brahma', which means 'the sun (that we see) is Brahman'. Of course, for Hindus the entire universe is Brahman, but the sun is the most powerful appearance of it, so it is used by Hindus as a symbol of Brahman.

Meditation

In old age some Hindus give up worldly ties. They have fulfilled their religious and social duties, and can now devote their remaining lives completely to God. They often practise meditation. Meditation (**Dhyana**) is based on a system of philosophy called yoga, which is explained in the Yoga Sutras. Yoga is practised to free the soul from a long cycle of birth, death and rebirth, allowing it to become one with the Supreme Spirit, Brahman. Freedom may be achieved in different ways – through the yoga of knowledge; of work; of complete devotion to God; by repeating the

This man is using a metal pot with a spout to enable him to make a continuous offering of water while he chants the Gayatri prayer to the sun.

This man is in deep meditation near the River Ganges. The Trident, God Shiva's weapon, placed near him indicates that he is a worshipper of Shiva.

Sacred Syllable **aum** or a mantra; and through the Hatha Yoga, which aims to direct the mind towards God through physical exercises. Yoga must be learned from a **guru** to avoid physical and spiritual harm.

The Sacred Syllable aum

NEW WORDS

Aum the Sacred Syllable of Hinduism, a word for God

Dhyana deep meditation

Guru a teacher who guides his followers on spiritual and religious questions

'My spirit is much grieved in Thy absence; come to me, O my Beloved Lord!
…Vain is my life! I have no taste for food: my eyes get no slumber.
I am restless within doors and without.
As water to the thirsty, so is the sight of the Lover to the bride:…
I am dying for sight of my Lord!'

(Kabir, 14th century)

The Sense of Sin

'Lord, I have abandoned all for Thee,
Yet evermore desire riseth in my heart,
And maketh me forget Thy love:
Ah, save me, save me,
Save me by Thyself:
As thus I bow before Thee, Lord,
Come dwell within,
Live Thou Thy secret life in me,
And save me by Thyself.'

(Tukaram, an Indian mystic, 1608–49)

4 Worship in the home

This unit tells you how worship is offered to murtis, or pictures of gods or goddesses, in the home shrine.

Worship in Hinduism takes many forms, such as repeating the holy names of God, walking around a murti or a shrine, listening to the words of a holy book and offering water to the sun, but the most common form of worship is called **puja**, when various offerings are made to a murti representing some quality of Brahman. A murti is an aid to worship. Puja is performed with whatever materials are available, and may be simple or elaborate.

Scriptures such as the Puranas and the Sutras form the basis of Hindu worship. The most important Sutra text is called the Ashwalayana Grihya Sutra (200 BCE). This gives the order of rituals, concise rules and mantras for performing puja and the various **samskaras** (life-cycle rituals).

Simple puja

The photograph (below) shows a very simple puja performed by a girl using flowers, water, incense sticks and oil lamps. Women are usually unable to chant mantras from the sacred texts when doing a puja at a home shrine, because they are not given the opportunity to learn them.

Detailed puja

Here is a description of a detailed sixteen-stage puja by a Hindu girl in London.

'My name is Asha. Last summer my elder brother got married and to give thanks to our family god, Vishnu, for our good fortune, my father decided to perform a detailed puja. We chose a Saturday because I had no school that day and Dad was also free. We all got up very early and bathed. Dad set up a shrine in the living room. We had no breakfast, only a cup of tea. The priest came at 8 o'clock. My Dad

Most Hindu homes contain a shrine which may be in the kitchen or a bedroom. This shrine is in a home in north India. It has pictures of God Hanuman, God Krishna and the Goddess Durga. There is also a picture of a local warrior from the past. A home shrine may also contain murtis and Ganges water in a sealed copper bottle.

performed the puja while the priest chanted the mantras in Sanskrit, and also explained each stage in English. The **deity**, in the form of a murti, was treated as an honoured guest and offerings were made as described in a holy book.

1. God was invited to be in the murti.
2. He was offered a seat.
3. He was offered water for washing the feet.
4. God was welcomed.
5. He was offered a drink of water.
6. The murti was placed in a copper dish and bathed with water and a little milk.
7. The murti was dried, placed in the copper dish in the shrine and dressed in a soft cotton-wool garland.
8. A sacred thread was put on the murti.
9. Dad applied sandalwood paste and red and yellow powders to the murti's forehead.
10. Flowers were arranged around it.
11. A lighted incense stick was waved before it.
12. A **ghee** lamp was offered.
13. A special semolina sweet and some fruit were offered.
14. Betel leaves were also offered.
15. Dad walked round the murti.
16. Finally, standing before it, Dad put the palms of his hands together and bowed to offer **namaskara**.

A woman doing arati at the end of a puja in a temple.

After the priest had chanted the final prayer we all received some semolina sweet as **prasad**. This puja took nearly an hour.'

NEW WORDS

Deity a god or goddess

Ghee clarified butter

Namaskara a greeting made by putting the palms of the hands together and bowing

Prasad blessed offering

Puja the most common form of worship

Samskara sacrament; a life-cycle ritual such as a baby's naming ceremony, the sacred thread ceremony, marriage or cremation

A prayer at the end of a puja
'Grant me, O Lord, a healthy appearance, success in my work and destroy my enemies. May I be blessed with sons, riches and all creature comforts.'
'You are my mother and father, my brother and friend. You are my knowledge and my strength. You are indeed my entire existence, O Lord.'
'Whatever actions I perform with my body, speech, mind and other sense-organs, whatever I do knowingly or indeed as a habit, I offer it all, without any reservations, to Narayana.' (From the Puranas)

5 Growing up in Hinduism

This unit explains how the words and the order of rituals given in the Grihya Sutras are used in a boy's initiation into the religious responsibilities of an adult Hindu.

Upanayana (the sacred thread ceremony) is the beginning of a boy's religious status as an adult Hindu. The ceremony marks the end of childhood and the start of the disciplined student stage in the life of a Hindu boy. After the ceremony the boy can represent his family in religious rituals. In the past only boys from the three upper **varnas** (social groups) experienced upanayana, but today some girls in progressive families also go through this important samskara.

Normally in India eight- to twelve-year-old boys undergo this ceremony, but in Britain even young men in their early twenties are prepared for the sacrament to preserve their religious tradition.

A personal experience

Here's how one Hindu describes what happened at a thread ceremony in India.

'Two years ago, I attended a thread ceremony in a Hindu home in Bombay. The priest followed the order of rituals and used the mantras as laid down in a Grihya Sutra text. He then arranged the various materials and a metal container for the sacred fire, while the boy and his parents bathed and got

A mother and her son eat together just before the ceremony. This is their spiritual 'goodbye', because from now on the boy will come more and more under the influence of his teacher, probably the family priest, and the older men of his family.

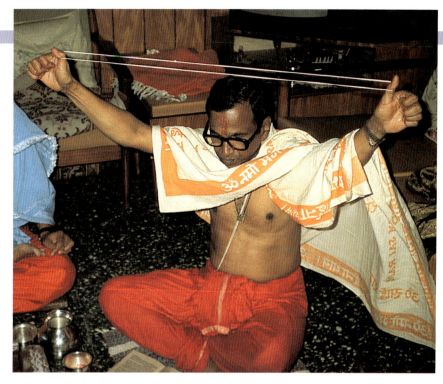

A priest blessing the sacred thread.

ready. First the mother and son ate together, after which the mother took no further part in the ceremony. Prayers and worship were offered to the family deities and the God Ganesha. The priest chanted mantras from the Rig-Veda and a Sutra text as he directed both father and son through various rituals. Prayers and worship were offered to the Sun God for inspiration, to Agni (God of Fire) for understanding, and to Palasha (a medicinal plant) for increasing intelligence. Then the priest blessed the sacred thread and asked the boy to wear it over his left shoulder and under his right arm, telling him that the thread would make him strong and healthy, and that it would be renewed every year in August. Then the boy's father taught his son to recite the Gayatri verse as a token start to his study of the scriptures. The boy was told to pay attention to his school work, to obey his teachers, and not to smoke, or eat or drink anything harmful. At the end of the ceremony the boy took up his Palasha staff and made as if to go off on a journey to his teacher's house but he didn't actually leave home. His parents and grandparents offered him food for the journey. In earlier times the boy really did go to stay with his guru until he had finished his studies.'

NEW WORDS

Upanayana the sacred thread ceremony

Varna a social group. The four traditional varnas in Hindu society are Brahmin (priests, professionals), Kshatriya (administrators, soldiers), Vaishya (business people) and Shudra (farm labourers, artisans)

Upanayana mantras

The father and son make offerings of ghee to Agni, the God of Fire, while the priest recites these mantras.

'We offer this prayer to Agni established here for the religious sacrificial ritual, who is all-seeing God as well as the purifier and the benefactor of the people. I give this offering to Agni, the Purifier.'

'O Agni, you perform praiseworthy deeds. Grant me wealth, sustenance, energy, and alertness of mind and intellect. I give this offering to Agni, the purifier.'

(Rig-Veda: 9.66–20,21)

6 The Vedas: the earliest holy books

This unit is about the earliest Hindu scriptures and how they were preserved through oral tradition.

The sacred nature of the Veda

Hindus firmly believe that the Veda was revealed by God. The divine words of God Brahman were heard by men who were inspired by them and composed the hymns about 3500 years ago. Because this eternal wisdom was heard, these sacred scriptures are known as **shruti**, which is Sanskrit for 'heard'. All later scriptures based on remembered tradition are known as **smriti** texts.

The content of the Veda

The term Veda (wisdom) includes four separate collections of verses and prose, called Rig-Veda, Sama-Veda, Yajur-Veda and Atharva-Veda. The Rig-Veda, the most important scripture, has over a thousand hymns praising different gods who control the forces of nature. The Sama-Veda refers to melodies, the Yajur-Veda deals with fire rituals and the Atharva-Veda describes magical spells.

Each of these four Vedas has four sections. They are Samhita, Brahmana, Aranyaka and Upanishad. The Samhita and Brahmana sections deal with the performance of worship. The later parts of each Veda, called

A priest reading a Vedic text in a temple.

Aranyaka and Upanishad, are concerned with the philosophy of devotion.

The oral tradition

In the past young boys and some girls would have learned to utter the correct sounds of the Rig-Veda by listening carefully to their teacher as he chanted the hymns. They had to hear every word and every line, and repeat them many times until they mastered the sounds. The hymns were not written down, so the pupils could not see the words in script; their only source of knowledge was the sound of their teacher's voice. He, too, would have learned the hymns from his teacher by word of mouth. The pupils learned the scriptures off by heart and, in turn, passed on their knowledge orally to the next generation, but the tradition of teaching girls the holy scriptures gradually lapsed, since they did not act as priests. The earliest sacred texts were preserved through oral tradition for centuries before they were written down. Now they are available in print in Sanskrit. Some portions are translated into Indian regional languages and into English.

Two extracts from the Rig-Veda

To Prithivi (Goddess of Earth):

'(Goddess) Earth, you bear the burden of heavy mountains, and with your many rivers you nourish the soil, Powerful One. These flowers of our songs resound in your praise. You send us the water-laden cloud, O shining Goddess. With your strength, you hold the trees firmly in the ground when the lightning flashes and thunder-rain showers from the sky.'   (Rig-Veda: 5. 84. 1–3.)

The sacrifice of Primal Man
– the **Purusha-Sukta**:

'From the performance of the complete sacrifice of the Primal Man (Purusha) arose the first three Vedas and the metres of the Vedas. From it also arose horses and other animals with teeth in either jaw, like sheep, cattle and goats. When they split up Primal Man, into how many parts was he divided? What did his mouth, arms, thighs and feet represent? The Brahmin was his mouth, the Kshatriya his arms, the Vaishya his thighs and the Shudra were born from his feet.'
        (Rig-Veda: 10. 90. 9–12.)

NEW WORDS

Purusha-Sukta a hymn describing the sacrifice of Primal Man

Shruti scriptures 'revealed' by God and 'heard' by sages

Smriti scriptures based on 'remembered tradition'

'In the beginning this world was Brahman, the limitless One – limitless to the east, limitless to the south, limitless to the west, limitless to the north, and above and below, limitless in every direction. Truly, for him east and the other directions exist not, nor across, nor below, nor above.

'Incomprehensible is that supreme Soul, unlimited, unborn, not to be reasoned about, unthinkable – He whose soul is space! In the dissolution of the world He alone remains awake. From that space He, assuredly, awakes this world, which is a mass of thought. It is thought by Him, and in Him it disappears.

'His is that shining form which gives heat in yonder sun and which is the brilliant light in a smokeless fire, as also the fire in the stomach which cooks food. For thus has it been said: "He who is in the fire, and he who is here in the heart, and he who is yonder in the sun – he is one."'
        (Maitri Upanishad)

7 Worship in a Hindu temple

This unit tells you how the words and the order of rituals given in a Purana text are used in worship in a Hindu temple.

The daily puja in a temple is normally performed by male priests, who are usually the only people allowed to enter the inner shrine. Appropriate mantras are chanted at each ritual. At festival times, all worshippers can enter the inner shrine and make offerings to the murti.

A personal experience

Here is one Hindu's account of puja at a temple.

'I travelled to a small town in western India to visit Vasant, a school friend. He is a teacher and his father, **Pandit** Gopal, is the chief priest at the local Vishnu temple. In the morning, after bathing, I went to the temple with Pandit Gopal and his assistant to attend the morning puja. There were about a dozen men and women waiting in the temple hall.

A priest doing a puja to a goddess.

We all witnessed the whole procedure.

1 Pandit Gopal and his assistant rang the bell at the entrance of the temple to announce their presence and opened the doors to the inner shrine.
2 The previous day's flowers and clothes on the murti were removed and the shrine was cleaned.
3 The murti was bathed with cold water and dried. As various offerings were made, Pandit Gopal chanted the appropriate mantra in Sanskrit.
4 The forehead of the murti was anointed with sandalwood paste, red kum-kum and yellow turmeric powders.
5 The murti was dressed in new clothes and fresh flower garlands.
6 The assistant priest lit incense sticks and a ghee lamp which Pandit Gopal waved in front of the murti.
7 A small metal bowl of fresh milk was placed in front of the murti. Some sliced coconut and sugar crystals were offered to God and received back as prasad (blessed offerings).
8 Pandit Gopal then performed the **arati** using a tray with a ghee lamp and ignited camphor oil tablets. The arati tray was waved in front of the murti while verses of praise were sung by everyone present.
9 When the tray was brought into the hall of the temple, people received the warmth of the sacred light and God's blessing.
10 Pandit Gopal walked in a clockwise direction around the murti in reverence.
11 He then joined his hands in the namaskara greeting in front of the murti.
12 Pandit Gopal and his assistant distributed prasad among those present.

(The evening puja is attended by many more people. At night the doors of the inner shrine are closed.)

On our way back, Pandit Gopal told me that temple worship was a very ancient tradition, though the rules for puja in a temple were written down in a scripture called Brahma Purana only about 600 years ago. "Are these rules followed in every temple?" I asked. "No," he replied, "they are altered according to the needs of different temples and in different regions of India."'

In Britain, the puja ceremony at a Hindu temple is important for instructing children in their religious tradition.

The following is a prayer from the Puranas usually recited at the beginning of a puja.

'For success in all actions I first praise Vinayaka (Ganesha), my Guru, the Sun God, Brahma, Vishnu, Shiva and Saraswati.

'Homage to God Ganesha, remover of all obstacles, worshipped by both Gods and Demons in order to attain their desires.

'May Brahma, Shiva and Vishnu, the Lords of the three worlds, make us successful in everything.'

NEW WORDS

Arati a ritual performed with a ghee lamp and ignited camphor

Pandit a Hindu priest; a learned man

'When I am worshipped in an icon, bathing Me and decorating Me are welcome...When worshipped in the sun, adoration by prostration, offering of water with mantras, muttering of prayer are best.... Some water offered to Me with love by a devotee pleases Me. Elaborate offerings, sandal, incense, flowers, light, food, made by one who is devoid of devotion, do not satisfy Me.'

(From the Bhagavata-Purana)

8 Religious teachers: gurus

This unit is about gurus, their place in different sects in Hinduism, and the Upanishads as the teachings of ancient gurus.

Guru

A Pandit performs rituals and ceremonies, but a guru is a religious teacher who guides his followers in developing their spiritual life. He has no family ties and very few possessions. He devotes his time to meditation and the study of Hindu philosophy in the Upanishads, which help him to find answers to his followers' problems. There is a long guru tradition in Hinduism. Many Hindus from different walks of life have a particular guru whose spiritual advice comforts them in times of distress.

Guru in a Hindu sect

The founder and first guru of each Hindu sect is a god or a goddess, and the living guru, the head of the sect, is believed to have received divine inspiration from God. He can initiate others into the sect. His experienced guidance shows the way to the true meaning of life. When a new leading guru takes over headship of a sect he has to be initiated by the previous guru.

Dr Anuragi (left), a guru.

The Upanishads as the teachings of ancient gurus

The Upanishads are discussions between ancient gurus and their chosen pupils about the meaning of life. They were composed towards the end of the shruti scriptures to explain the nature of Brahman, **atman** (individual soul), the universe, the effect of actions (**karma**), how the soul exists through a cycle of successive births and deaths, how the soul can achieve freedom from successive lives, and the one-ness of things throughout the created universe.

Extracts from the Upanishads

Selfless action:

'This whole universe is pervaded by Ishwara, God. Be content with whatever is your lot and do not desire things that belong to others. By performing various religious rituals and carrying out duties according to one's **dharma**, one should live for a hundred years. It is not possible to give up all activity, but when actions are done as a duty, the burden of karma does not attach to the individual soul.' (From the Isha Upanishad, verses 1 and 2.)

The following story shows the one-ness of God Brahman, atman, the individual soul and the universe.

'Uddalaka said to his son, Svetaketu, "Put this salt in a beaker of water." Svetaketu did as he was told. Next morning his father said, "Svetaketu, my son, bring the beaker of water and take out the salt." "I can't see the salt" he replied, bringing the beaker. "Now," said Uddalaka, "take sips from opposite sides of the beaker and describe the taste." "The water tastes of salt from both sides" replied Svetaketu. "My son," said Uddalaka, "though you do not see it, the salt is there. Similarly you do not perceive that finest essence, the universal soul, yet it is here. That, my son, is the Final Reality. That is atman, and you also

are that essence."' (From Chhandogya Upanishad: 6. 13. 1–3.)

'Without doubt Brahman exists in two states: with form and formless, the mortal and the immortal, the still and the moving, the actual and the incomprehensible.'
(From Brihad Aranyaka Upanishad:2. 3. 1.)

NEW WORDS

Atman the individual soul

Dharma social and religious duty of a person according to his or her varna (social group), stage in life and occupation

Karma the consequences of action; also action or work

'People say: "A person is made [not of acts, but] of desires only." [In reply to this I say:] As is his desire, such is his resolve; as is his resolve, such the action he performs; whatever action he performs determines what he shall be.'   (Brihadaranyaka Upanishad)
'Know God, and all chains will be loosed. Ignorance will vanish. Birth, death, and rebirth will be no more. Meditate upon him…. Thus will you reach union with the lord of the universe. Thus will you become identified with him who is One…. In him all your desires will find fulfilment.'   (Svetasvatara Upanishad)

9 The story of a war

This unit is about the quarrel between the Pandavas and their cousins, the Kauravas, which led to a war which the Pandavas won.

Why did the war happen?

Long ago at Hastinapur in India there lived two princes: Dhritarashtra, who was blind from birth, and his younger brother, Pandu.

When their father died, Pandu became king because his elder brother was blind. When Pandu died after a short reign, Dhritarashtra became king, since Pandu's five sons, the Pandavas, were very young.

Dhritarashtra was married to Gandhari. They had many sons, known as the Kauravas. The eldest of them was Duryodhana. The

God Ganesha writing the Mahabharata.

Kauravas and the Pandavas lived in the same palace and were trained in the art of warfare by the same teachers. The Pandavas became skilful in the use of weapons, which made the Kauravas furious.

Dhritarashtra was ambitious for his eldest son, Duryodhana, and wanted to make him his heir. But the senior men at court favoured Yudhishthir, the eldest Pandava. The king reluctantly gave in and Yudhishthir was made Crown Prince. The Kauravas became more jealous and quarrelled with the Pandavas. Now Dhritarashtra divided the kingdom equally. He gave the poor half to the Pandavas and kept the capital, Hastinapur, for himself and his sons. The Pandavas built a new capital in their half of the kingdom and prospered.

Duryodhana, supported by his mother's brother, tricked Yudhishthir into a gambling match. Yudhishthir fell for it, gambled heavily and lost everything. The Pandavas went into exile as a forfeit for thirteen years. At the end of their exile they demanded their half of the kingdom, which Duryodhana refused to give them. They pleaded for their just and rightful share but got nowhere. War became inevitable.

Both sides gathered large armies and faced each other on the field of Kurukshetra. Arjuna, the Pandava prince, did not wish to kill his kinsmen, so he refused to fight. God Krishna, acting as Arjuna's charioteer, pointed out that as a warrior it was Arjuna's varna duty to fight. When Arjuna was convinced, the war started. It lasted for eighteen days and claimed thousands of lives. The Kauravas were killed in battle. The Pandavas won, but at a terrible price.

The sacred text

This story forms the central theme of a poem called the Mahabharata, which is the longest in the world. It has 100,000 verses arranged in 18 books. Along with the central theme, many other stories in it stress the importance of religious, social and moral duties. Here is one of them.

'Though his blind father had lost his kingdom, Princess Savitri married Prince Satyawan who was slowly dying. When Yama, God of Death, came for him, Savitri begged for Satyawan's life so sincerely that Yama granted her one wish. Savitri said: "May my father-in-law see his grandson on the throne of his kingdom." Yama agreed and realised he had been tricked by Savitri's loyalty and faith: Satyawan would live; he and Savitri would have a son who would rule the restored kingdom; and the old King's sight would return.'

Some moral lessons from the central theme

1 Arjuna did not wish to kill his kinsmen, so he refused to fight. Krishna pointed out to him that as a warrior it was his duty to fight, since varna duty takes priority over other considerations.
2 The Pandavas fought a righteous war for their just cause, but only as a last resort.
3 Because the blind king put his son's ambition above his duty to the state, death and destruction resulted.
4 Gambling brought utter ruin to the noble prince Yudhishthir.
5 Jealousy cost the Kauravas their lives and kingdom.

'Dharma is the foundation of the whole universe.... By means of dharma one drives away evil. Upon dharma everything is founded. Therefore, dharma is called the highest good.'   (Taittiriya Aranyaka, 10.79)

'For the sake of the promotion of strength and efficacy among beings the declaration of dharma is made. Whatever is attended with nonviolence (ahimsa), that is dharma. Such is the fixed opinion.'

(Mahabharata 12.110.10)

10 Ganesha worship in the Puranas

This unit shows that Ganesha worship and the origin of his murti are based on the Purana texts.

The murti of Ganesha

The Ganesha murti is based on the stories in six different Puranas. Ganesha has a human body and an elephant's head, indicating that all beings are created by Brahman. He has only one tusk. He rides on a mouse, showing God's concern for all creatures, great and small. He has four hands. He holds an axe and a goad in the top right hand. The axe is to remove obstacles and the goad is to keep his devotees on the path of dharma, religious and social duty. The snare in the top left hand shows his control over death. In his bottom left hand he holds a sweetmeat, representing a reward for devotion, and with his lower right hand he blesses his devotees. He wears a snake around his waist.

Ganesha worship

God Ganesha is believed to remove obstacles from any human activity. He is widely worshipped by Hindus daily, and at the start of religious rituals such as the sacred thread ceremony and marriage. Prayers are offered to him on a child's first day at school or at the start of a journey. A prayer from a Purana

A Ganesha murti in a temple in London. This Ganesha murti does not hold the symbols in his hands.

text commonly used in a puja says:

> 'O God (Ganesha), possessing an elephant's head, a large (human) body and the brightness of many suns, remove all obstacles from all my tasks, always, I beg.'

Many Hindu homes have a Ganesha murti or a picture, often near the front door, so that Ganesha may be greeted with namaskara on entry and when leaving, in thanks for a safe journey or in the hope that there will be no problems on the way home.

There are many stories about Ganesha in the Puranas. Here is one of them:

> 'Once, Parvati, God Shiva's wife, made a little figure of a boy with an elephant's head out of some herbal ointment and threw it into the River Ganges. Through the divine power of the river goddess, the figure came to life. Parvati considered the boy her son, since she had given him form, but Ganga also claimed that she was his mother, since she had given him life. Because both Parvati and Ganga claimed him as their son, he is called "Dwaimatura" in Sanskrit, which means "the one who has two mothers". God Shiva made him the leader of his semi-divine attendants (the Ganas). That is how he came to be called Ganesha.' (From Matsya Purana.)

An ancient popular belief

The author and editor ('arranger') of the Mahabharata is believed to have dictated the entire story to Ganesha, who wrote it down in its present form (see Unit 9). Ganesha therefore has a reputation as a writer and scholar.

Ganesha festival

This annual festival is celebrated in August in India and in many Hindu homes in Britain. The public festival was revived in 1892 to unite Indians in their political struggle against British rule. Here is one child's account of the festival in a letter to his uncle.

'Dear Uncle,
Two weeks after you left Nasik and returned to England, we celebrated the Ganesha festival. Every household paid 100 rupees to the area festival committee and many boys and girls helped to decorate the pavilion. The first day's puja was done by a rich shopowner. I think by giving him that honour, the committee managed to get a 1000 rupee donation from him.

On the first day our lunch was a real feast. We all enjoyed the evening arati and prasad on all ten days. In the evenings there were song contests, mostly Hindi film songs, and **bhajans**. The final afternoon's puja was done by our headmaster, so the school closed early. The last day's procession of all the murtis from different areas took four hours to reach the river, because many people along the way were offering flowers to murtis. Then there were the drum players and team dancers. After the final arati near the river, we all touched the feet of the clay murti before it was put in the river. It really was a most enjoyable festival.

With regards,
your nephew, Anand.'

NEW WORD

Bhajan a devotional hymn sung as a chorus with music

'We call upon you, Ganesha, the leader of the assembly of Gods, the divine priest, the scholar among scholars, first among the knowers of Brahman, of incomparable fame. Hear our prayer and grace this place with your all-protecting presence.'

(Rig-Veda: 2.23.1)

11 Worship of Goddess Durga in the Puranas

This unit tells you how the Goddess Durga and her worship originated in the Purana texts.

Hindu belief in God begins with the Veda, which is the word of God. Although the Rig-Veda praises many 'gods', there is a firm belief that these different 'gods' are aspects of One Truth – the Highest God. Brahma, Vishnu and Shiva have their origins in the Rig-Veda. Later gods of Hinduism such as Ganesha are first mentioned in the Puranas. Gods are prominent in Vedic scriptures, but in later Hinduism goddesses begin to be worshipped with equal reverence. After the 9th century CE Goddess Durga became well known. Three important Puranas (Vishnu, Skanda and Markandeya) tell stories about her and encourage her worship. Devi Purana and Kalika Purana describe her worship. In modern Hinduism the Mother Goddess is known by various names such as Maha Lakshmi, Parvati, Amba, Kali and the Warrior Goddess Durga.

The Devi Mahatmya in the Markandeya Purana says:

> 'Durga pervades the world. She creates, maintains and destroys it as the need arises. Although Durga is eternal, she appears again and again to protect the world. She supports and shelters all beings. As 'shakambhari', she provides the world with food.'

The Durga murti

The Durga murti shows a beautiful ten-armed warrior goddess riding a lion and holding several weapons, including Vishnu's discus and Shiva's trident. In her commonly found stone murti, she is shown as killing the buffalo demon Mahisha; this story is told in the Markandeya Purana.

A woman worshipping the Goddess Durga in the inner shrine.

Final puja of the Goddess at the end of the festival.

'A demon named Mahisha performed many acts of worship and penance and obtained the blessing that he would be able to defeat all enemies except a woman. Mahisha defeated the gods and became a threat to the world. The gods in their helplessness created, from their energy, a beautiful woman, Durga, and gave her their weapons. She attacked Mahisha, who had assumed the form of a fearsome buffalo, and killed him, making the world safe for gods and humans. When Durga fought and killed the demon Mahisha, she was not assisted by any god. Durga appeared on two more occasions to help destroy evil demons and protect the world.' (From Devi Mahatmya in Markandeya Purana.)

The festival

The Durga puja festival is celebrated during the nine days of Navaratri in October and November, in a similar way to the Ganesha festival (see Unit 10). A specially made murti of Durga is offered morning and evening puja, followed by arati and prasad. On the eighth day a special puja is offered; then, on the ninth, the murti is taken in procession to the sea or the local river, where it is placed in the water.

'Whatever I speak is the muttering of Your prayer; all art is the symbol of Your worship; all my movement is going round You in honour; eating, etc., is making offerings to You; if I lie down it is prostration to You; all my enjoyments are in a spirit of dedication to You; O Goddess! whatever I do may it be a synonym of Your worship.'

(Shankara, Saundaryalahari, 27)

12 A tyrant king is punished

This unit describes how God Vishnu took human form to punish the cruel and unjust King Kamsa.

God Vishnu is believed to have appeared on Earth in several forms, not all of them human, to protect people from such evils as a wicked king or a powerful demon. God's appearance on Earth as saviour is called an **avatar** (incarnation). Nine such avatars have taken place and the tenth and last is yet to come. God **Krishna** is Vishnu's eighth avatar.

The fast and feast of God Krishna's birthday

Hindus celebrate God Krishna's birth in August or September. Many people observe a fast during the 24 hours before the day itself. In Krishna (Vishnu) temples, priests read the birth story from scriptures called the Bhagavata Purana or the Harivamsha. Listening to the words of the text on this night is an act of devotion. The following day is celebrated as a prasad feast, when special sweet dishes are served for lunch.

Here is the story of Krishna from the scriptures:

Krishna's birth

'Ugrasena, the king of Mathura, had a son called Kamsa and a daughter named Devaki. Kamsa imprisoned his father and began to rule the kingdom very harshly. When Devaki was married to Prince Vasudeva, her brother Kamsa, who was driving their chariot in the wedding procession, heard a heavenly voice saying that he would be killed by Devaki's eighth child. Immediately, Devaki and Vasudeva were imprisoned and kept there for many years. As time went on, Kamsa oppressed his subjects and caused much misery. Six of Devaki's children disappeared as soon as they were born, and the seventh was rescued through a miracle.

When Devaki was pregnant for the eighth time, Kamsa ordered the prison guards to be extra watchful. On a dark and stormy night during the monsoons, Devaki's eighth child, a son, was born in the form of God Krishna. Immediately the baby assumed a grown-up form, revealed himself to Vasudeva as an incarnation of God Vishnu and told him how he could be rescued from prison. After Krishna had become a baby again, Vasudeva placed him in a basket, and covered it to keep the baby warm. The guards seemed to be asleep; the locks gave way and the gates opened by themselves and Vasudeva, carrying baby Krishna, walked to the River Yamuna. As if by a miracle, the river water divided, allowing Vasudeva to cross over to the house of a cowherd chief, Nanda. Nanda's wife, Yashoda, had given birth to a daughter at exactly the same time as God Krishna was born. Vasudeva

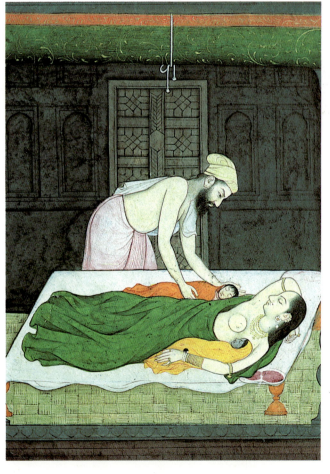

The exchange of the babies.

exchanged the babies and walked back to the prison with the baby girl, unseen by anyone.

When he was inside the cell, the baby girl in Devaki's arms began to cry loudly. The guards woke up from their slumber and saw the cell secured as before. They informed Kamsa of the birth of the child. Kamsa came to the prison and snatched the girl from Devaki. The baby girl, who was also a divine being, escaped from Kamsa's hand and, informing him that his enemy was safe in Nanda's house, disappeared.'

The tyrant Kamsa is killed

'Krishna grew up in his foster parents' house and spent his early years in the company of other boys and girls. His favourite friend was a milkmaid called Radha.

A serpent named Kaliya lived in the River Yamuna near the village, poisoning its waters and threatening the lives of the villagers and their cattle. Krishna saved many lives by taming Kaliya and extracting a promise from him not to poison the waters. On another occasion he rescued the cowherds and their cattle from a flood.

Kamsa had tried to find Krishna in Nanda's village, but Krishna managed to escape. A few years later Krishna was invited to the capital, where he killed the tyrant Kamsa, rescued Vasudeva and Devaki and restored the old king Ugrasena to the throne, thus removing injustice and suffering.'

(From the Bhagavata Purana.)

Young Krishna and Radha.

All in Krishna, Krishna in all
God Krishna speaks:
'O Arjuna, see my hundreds and thousands of different forms, some divine, all displaying a variety of shapes and colours.'
'Behold the deities of light, of wind, and of storms. See the guardians of the eight directions, the heavenly twins, and many wonders never seen before.'
'And Arjuna, now behold, centred in my body, the whole universe, including moving and fixed things, and whatever else you wish to see.'   (The Bhagavad-Gita: 11. 5–7)

NEW WORDS

Avatar God's appearance on Earth to protect the good and punish and destroy the evil. An incarnation

Krishna God Vishnu's eighth and most important avatar

13 The Bhagavad-Gita

This unit tells you about a widely read scripture, the Bhagavad-Gita.

It is well known for many reasons. It is written in simple Sanskrit and the printed text is easily available. There is a message for all people to help them deal with life's problems and to bring them spiritual comfort. The Bhagavad-Gita emphasizes the importance of doing one's duty to the best of one's ability and having complete faith in the supreme God Krishna. It has been translated into all major Indian languages, and English.

The story

Unit 9 told of a terrible battle between the armies of the Pandavas and the Kauravas at a place called Kurukshetra in northern India. Hindus know the story well because one of their favourite scriptures, the Bhagavad-Gita, is based on it.

God Krishna had agreed to act as the Pandava prince Arjuna's charioteer. As the armies lined up for battle, Arjuna asked Krishna to drive up and down the battlefield in the space between the armies. As he saw the thousands of men on both sides of him, he thought how many of them would be killed that day. Many might be his relatives. Arjuna was filled with horror and asked Krishna to take him away from the battlefield. He would not fight. Krishna told him that he must. He was a member of the warrior (Kshatriya) varna. It was his duty to fight in a just cause. If he won he would gain his kingdom; if he was killed in battle he would go to heaven, gain spiritual freedom (**moksha**) and not be reborn.

God Krishna and Prince Arjuna in a chariot on the battlefield of Kurukshetra.

These are some of the words which Krishna spoke:

> 'You have a right to act, but never to the rewards of action; never let reward be the reason for your actions; yet you should not try to avoid action.' (Chapter 2. 47.)

> 'To protect the righteous, to destroy the wicked and to establish new order (dharma), I incarnate Myself from age to age.' (Chapter 4. 8.)

> 'Whoever with devotion and a pure mind offers Me even a leaf, a flower, a fruit or a little water, that sincere and loving offering I accept.' (Chapter 9. 26.)

> 'By taking refuge in Me, O Arjuna, women, merchants (Vaishya) and artisans (Shudra), though lowly born (and having a low social status), also reach the highest goal (i.e. attain moksha).' (Chapter 9. 32.)

> 'Forsaking all other paths, take refuge only in Me: I will release you from all sins. Do not grieve.' (Chapter 18. 66.)

Arjuna obeyed Krishna. The battle was fought and the Pandavas won.

The text

The Bhagavad-Gita dates from about 250CE, has 700 verses arranged in 18 chapters and takes about three hours to recite. In some Krishna temples in India, it is read aloud continuously, day and night, for a week immediately before the celebration of Krishna's birth festival. Many Hindus read a few verses every day because it is the word of God.

The message

Some important ideas in the scripture are:

1 A person's soul is eternal and never dies. Hindus call the soul atman.
2 The Supreme Spirit, Brahman, fills the entire universe.
3 The soul and the Supreme Spirit are identical. They may blend together like drops of water in a river, or as rivers in the sea.
4 All actions should be performed as a duty and without any desire for reward.
5 God's avatars (bodily forms) appear on Earth to save people, to punish the wicked and to establish a new order based on justice.
6 The paths of wisdom, selfless action, complete devotion to God and meditation (yoga) are all ways which lead to spiritual freedom.
7 Krishna is the Supreme God. For his devotees he is the only refuge.
8 Devotion is more important in worship than expensive offerings.
9 All men and women, whatever their social status, can win moksha through Krishna.

NEW WORD

Moksha spiritual freedom of the soul

The true devotee of God

'He who has no ill will to any being, who is friendly and compassionate, free from egoism and self-sense, even-minded in pain and pleasure, and patient,
The Yogi who is ever content, self-controlled, unshakable in determination, with mind and understanding given up to Me – he, My devotee, is dear to Me.
He from whom the world does not shrink and who does not shrink from the world and who is free from joy and anger, fear and agitation – he too is dear to Me.'

(The Bhagavad-Gita: 12. 13–15)

14 The Ramayana

This unit tells you why the Ramayana is an important sacred text in the lives of many Hindus.

When the corpse of a Hindu is carried to the cremation ground, the mourners chant 'Ram bolo Ram. Jay Ram, jay Ram.' This means 'Speak the name of God Rama. Victory to Rama, victory to Rama.' This phrase is used in the hope that the deceased will get spiritual freedom.

Rama, Sita, Lakshmana and Hanuman.

The power of the name Rama

Millions of Hindus speak the name of God Rama when they get up in the morning and offer worship and prayers to Rama after bathing. When Hindus meet other Hindus, they greet each other by saying 'Ram-Ram'. A dying person is asked to say 'Ram-Ram' to gain religious merit. No other name of God has such a hold on the Hindu mind. Rama's birth festival is celebrated with special worship in March or April.

The Ramayana is a long poem in Sanskrit, believed to be the work of a poet named Valmiki. Its 24,000 verses are arranged in seven books. Rama, Sita and Lakshmana are the main characters and Rama is the seventh avatar of God Vishnu. The story has been translated into all major Indian languages, and these versions are considered sacred texts because they reach millions of people who do not know Sanskrit. In some Hindu temples in Britain, reading part of the text is a regular devotional activity.

The story portrays ideal characters. Rama is an obedient son, a dutiful king, a loving husband. Lakshmana is his affectionate and loyal brother. Hanuman is the ideal servant and Sugriva a trusted ally. Sita is the ideal faithful wife.

The story

King Dasharatha had three wives. The youngest queen, Kaikeyi, had once helped him win a battle. The King was very pleased and offered her any two things she wished, but she postponed her choice. When Dasharatha decided to make his eldest son, Rama, his heir, Queen Kaikeyi demanded the fulfilment of her two wishes. She asked that Rama be exiled for fourteen years and that her son, Bharata, be made heir to the throne. The King was speechless. His dream had been shattered, but he had given his word, and to honour it he agreed to the Queen's demands.

The people of Ayodhya, the capital, were preparing to greet their Crown Prince, Rama; instead they found themselves saying goodbye. Rama accepted his father's decision and prepared to leave the kingdom. His dutiful wife, Sita and brother, Lakshmana went with him. Soon afterwards, King Dasharatha died of grief for Rama. Bharata went to bring Rama back but failed. Bharata ruled in his brother's name during Rama's exile.

One day, while living in a far-off forest, Sita was kidnapped by Ravana, King of Lanka, while Rama and Lakshmana were away hunting. In their search for Sita, the brothers came to the kingdom of Sugriva, who agreed to help. Sugriva sent his trusted general, Hanuman, to look for Sita. Hanuman found her in captivity in Lanka. Rama, Lakshmana, Sugriva and Hanuman gathered a large army of monkeys, crossed the ocean and attacked Lanka. After a fierce battle Rama killed Ravana and rescued Sita.

Rama wondered whether Sita had been faithful all these years. She proved her faithfulness by walking on live coals and remaining unhurt. Rama, Sita, Lakshmana and Hanuman returned to Ayodhya, where Rama was crowned, to the delight of the people of the kingdom.

'My dear one! In this world, virtue, material gain, and pleasure are all to be found in the fruit gathered from the pursuit of virtue; I am sure they will all be found there even as in the case of a chaste wife who is also beloved and blessed with offspring. If there is a case in which the three are not found together, one should do only that in which there is virtue, for one who is intent solely on material gain is to be hated, and to be engrossed completely in pleasure is also not praiseworthy.'
'From dharma issue profit and pleasure; one attains everything by dharma, it is dharma which is the essence and strength of the world.'   (Ramayana 2.21.57–58; 3.9.30)

15 The Ramalila

This unit shows how stories from a Hindu scripture are presented as plays in the Ramalila celebrations.

The celebration of most Hindu festivals is based on the scriptures. Reading a scripture, listening to it as it is read aloud by a priest, or seeing the plays based on its stories, are different ways of continuing the religious tradition.

The festival of Ramalila takes place during the nine days of Navaratri in many places throughout northern India, including Delhi and Varanasi. Various stories from the Ramayana are acted out to entertain and inform the audience. The Ramalila plays convey the struggle between good and evil. This dramatic way of re-telling the Rama story is very popular and the performances are attended by Hindus, young and old, from all walks of life. Here are two of the stories from the scripture on which the plays are based.

Rama wins the archery contest:

'Many princes had assembled for an archery contest at the court of King Janaka. Prince Rama and his brother Lakshmana were among them. Janaka announced that whoever managed to string the mighty bow would marry his beautiful daughter, Sita. A murmur of wonder filled the court as a heavy bow was wheeled into the arena. Prince after prince tried, but no one could even lift the bow. Then Ravana, King of Lanka, came forward and, after much effort, lifted the bow. As he tried to bend it, he lost his balance and fell flat on his back with the heavy bow on top of

This elephant is carrying actors to the park, where they will take part in the performance of Ramalila.

32

him. As he struggled for breath on the floor, Sita laughed at him, which made him very angry. When many attendants had moved the bow to one side, Ravana went back to his seat, quite humiliated. Finally Rama came forward, lifted the bow easily and, as he tried to bend it, it broke in two. The assembled crowds rose to their feet as King Janaka declared Rama the winner of the contest. A few days later Rama and Sita were married.'

Ravana, his son and his brother are killed in battle:

'Rama collected an army of monkeys with the help of his friend King Sugriva and Sugriva's general Hanuman, and attacked Lanka. Many battles took place. In one battle, Lakshmana was badly injured, but the doctor cured him using medicinal herbs. In the final battle Ravana, his son and his brother were killed by Rama. Sita was rescued from her captivity. After Ravana's youngest brother was declared King of Lanka, Rama, Sita and Lakshmana returned to Ayodhya with Hanuman.'

The final destruction of Ravana, his son and his brother is acted out on the **Dasara** day, when their effigies, filled with fireworks, are set alight.

NEW WORD

Dasara the day after Navaratri

From a popular prayer to Rama
'May Rama, the descendant of King Raghu, protect my head.
May Rama, the son of King Dasharatha, protect my temples.
May Rama, the son of queen Kausalya, protect my eyes.
May Rama, the pupil of Vishwamitra, protect my ears.
May Rama, the affectionate brother of Lakshmana, protect my mouth.'

Effigies of Ravana, his son and his brother.

16 The scriptures and Hindu weddings

This unit tells you how the Hindu scriptures are used in weddings.

A Hindu wedding ceremony is based on the Ashwalayana Grihya Sutra text, which gives the rules of procedure, the correct order of rituals and the Sanskrit mantra for each ritual. In some regions of India the order of rituals is changed; this does not affect the ceremony. However, if two separate rituals are combined to produce a new ritual not mentioned in the scripture, a part of the ceremony becomes incorrect and creates confusion.

A personal experience

Here is how one Hindu describes what happened at a wedding in Britain:
'Anil and Anita are British-born Hindus and English is their first language. They do not know Sanskrit, but they wanted a full ceremony with the Sanskrit mantras from the scriptures. They repeated the mantras after

A bride and bridegroom walk the seven steps.

the priest to make their responses as he led them through ten parts of the ceremony, keeping carefully to the correct order.

1 Anita's parents offered puja to their family deities and God Ganesha.
2 Anil's family were received by Anita's parents at the door of the hall. Anil was given a little honey in welcome. At each ritual in the ceremony the priest chanted the appropriate mantra from the scriptures.
3 Anita was formally given in marriage. Anil promised Anita that he would be moderate in the practice of his dharma, **artha** and **kama**.
4 Verses of blessing were sung and the couple were showered with rice grains at the end of each verse.
5 The couple garlanded each other and showered each other with rice. Each tied a piece of soft cotton thread around the other's wrist. Anil then gave Anita her wedding necklace of black beads.
6 Anil took Anita's right hand and said the following mantra in Sanskrit:

'I take your hand, my bride, for good luck. May we grow old together. The Gods Bhaga, Aryaman, Surya and Indra have entrusted you to me as my life partner.'

(Rig-Veda 10. 85. 36.)

7 The marriage **homa** was performed. The couple made offerings of wood, ghee, grain and roasted millet to Agni (God of Fire) and walked around it in reverence, praying for children, health and long married life.
8 Then came the saptapadi ritual. Anil and Anita walked seven steps together in a line near the holy fire as the scriptures demanded. For each step Anil spoke the Sanskrit mantra:

'My bride, follow me in my vows. Take the first step for food...take the second step for strength...the third for increasing prosperity...the fourth for happiness...the fifth for children. May we have many healthy and long-lived sons. Take the sixth step for seasonal pleasures...take the seventh step for lifelong friendship.'

(Ashwalayana Grihya Sutra.)

9 The priest and senior members of both families blessed the couple.
10 That night Anil and Anita looked up at the Pole Star, promising to be constant to each other.

NEW WORDS

Artha, kama the bridegroom promises that he will be moderate in the practice of his dharma (religious and social duties), artha (earning money) and kama (enjoying the good things of life)

Homa a ritual in which offerings of wood, ghee and grain are made to Agni (God of Fire)

'O Agni, this wood fuel is your atman. May you burn vigorously because of it. May your power increase. Likewise, may our children, our cattle and our knowledge of Brahman increase. May we be blessed with plenty of food [and water] through your grace. I give you this fuel. Now that it is given to Agni, it is no longer mine.'

(A mantra for the Homa from Ashwalayana Grihya Sutra 1.10.12)

17 Scriptures in the lives of children (1)

This unit is about the use of scriptures in two separate religious rituals, performed when a baby is born, and when it is given a name.

Children are warmly welcomed in Hindu families. Their safe arrival is prayed for, and their welcome and caring entry to the family group are made clear by the many rituals found in the ancient scriptures which focus on a new baby's well-being.

A baby is born
The Grihya Sutra text by Ashwalayana says:

> 'When a baby is born its father should come to see it. He should bathe and put on clean clothes. Afterwards he offers prayers to God. Gently holding the baby in his lap, he should turn to the east and, using a gold ring, put a few drops of honey and ghee mixture in the baby's mouth. Then he should say: "Dear child, I give you this honey and ghee which is provided by God, who is the Creator of the world. May you be protected by God and live in this world for a hundred autumns. By God's grace may you become strong and firm like a rock, an axe for the wicked, and bright in character. May God give you long life and understanding of the Vedas."'

This ritual is performed mainly in devout Brahmin families. In the past, when most babies were born at home, the ritual could be done soon after birth. But today, in large cities, many babies are born in hospitals, so this ritual is performed as soon as the mother and child return home.

The naming of a child
With the giving of a name, the child becomes an individual personality in the family.
The Ashwalayana Grihya Sutra says:

> 'This sacrament of naming a baby should be performed on the 11th or 12th day after birth. The father should worship the family gods and goddesses before noon, with the help of the family priest. Rice grains should be spread on a metal plate and, using a gold ring, the chosen name should be written in the rice. Prayers are said so that the baby will be clever and healthy and grow up to be dutiful.'

A father and child after the naming ceremony.

The text recommends that:

'The name of a boy should be pleasing in sound and easy to say. Girls should be named after stars, such as Rohini, or after rivers, such as Ganga or Kaveri, or after birds, like the Maina.'

This religious ritual is performed mainly in devout Brahmin families, but many Hindus celebrate the occasion in the afternoon on the twelfth day by inviting relatives and friends. The baby is dressed in new clothes and placed in a cradle. Some families light twelve lamps and place them under the cradle. The chosen name of the baby is announced by the eldest woman in the family. Invited women with children sing cradle songs in which the baby's name is mentioned at the appropriate place. All guests then enjoy refreshments with special sweet dishes, prepared for the occasion.

In Britain, the naming of a baby is celebrated in many Hindu homes.

Worship of Shashthi devi
'In devout Brahmin families worship is offered to a minor aspect of the Mother Goddess, who protects a child before it is born and in its infancy. This goddess is called Shashthi devi (a name for Durga), and the worship is offered in the evening of the sixth day after the birth of a baby.
"O Goddess, you are the support of Gods and humans. I invoke your presence on this day. As you protected this mother and child during pregnancy, please protect them always, so that the child will have good health and long life through your grace."'

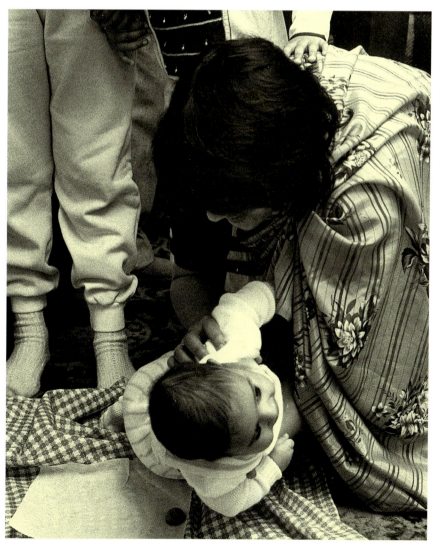

The naming of a Hindu baby.

This unit tells you how a baby's first outing, its first haircut and the custom of ear-piercing are based on scriptures.

Traditionally, Hindu babies do not have to face the outside world until they are thought to be strong and healthy enough to do so.

A baby's first outing

The Ashwalayana Grihya Sutra says:

> 'The first outing may take place in the third or fourth month after birth. It should be done on a day when the moon will be clearly visible after dark, as the baby is taken to see it. The parents and the baby should bathe and wear new clothes, then the baby's father should offer morning worship to the family gods. Afterwards the parents should take the child out of the house to show the little one the sun for a few seconds.'

This ritual is designed to make the child aware of the world outside. Many Hindus take their children to the local temple for their first outing so that they may receive God's blessing. A four-month-old baby is made aware of light, darkness, different colours and shapes through this ritual.

The piercing of ear lobes

The surgeon Sushruta claims in his Sutra text (350CE) that:

> 'Ear-piercing is to be done for two reasons. Firstly, it will enable the child to wear earrings. Secondly, it will make a child healthy, long-lived and well-to-do.'

A young woman wearing earings and a nose stud.

This sacrament has been faithfully followed by Hindus in order to make certain of these blessings.

Many Hindu children have their ear lobes pierced on the afternoon of the naming day by the local goldsmith. Both boys and girls have their ear lobes pierced when they are a few months old if the ritual is not carried out on the naming day. Girls have their left nostrils pierced, too, at the age of four or five years, so that they can wear nose ornaments.

In India older married women often wear an expensive nose ring made of pearls bound into an attractive design by gold wire.

A child's first haircut

The Sanskrit name for the first haircut is **Chaulam**. The Grihya Sutra of Paraskara says that this sacrament may be performed some time after the first birthday. Ashwalayana, on the other hand, insists that Chaulam is to be done in the third year. The Ashwalayana Grihya Sutra further recommends

'that the sacrament should be performed when the Sun has resumed its northerly course. On the day of the ritual a Homa should be performed and offerings of ghee and wood fuel made to Agni (God of Fire). Four earthenware pots filled with rice, barley, pulses and sesamum should be placed near the sacred fire. These are given to the barber as payment with some cash. After the Homa the child should be led away from the sacred fire and asked to sit in front of the barber. The father should sit behind the child, to give moral support.'

The Sutra text mentions the use of a razor, which suggests that the head is to be shaved completely.

The physician Charaka (about 180CE) in his medical text says:

'The trimming of nails, the cutting of hair and the shaving of the head promotes cleanliness,

good health and long life. Periodic shaving of the head keeps the scalp free of infection and encourages strong growth of hair.'

The ritual is experienced mainly by boys in devout Brahmin families, but in some parts of India very young girls also experience Chaulam. In modern practice very few young boys have their heads shaved; most people follow the European fashion. The child has a bath after the haircut and enjoys some special sweet dish at lunch.

NEW WORD

Chaulam a child's first haircut

Protection against evil spirits and the envious eye

There is a widespread belief that the ghost of a woman who dies in childbirth will cause physical and mental harm to a healthy child, particularly if it has a fair complexion. The 'envious eye' of a childless woman is also dangerous.

If a healthy baby suddenly becomes ill, a specialist priest is invited. He consecrates some wood ash by chanting a prayer to Vishnu or Shiva. The 'holy' ash is smeared on the child's forehead, shoulders, stomach, arms and legs.

A minor text recommends that a protective mantra written on a birch leaf be enclosed in an amulet tied to the child's arm.

19 Scriptures in regional languages (1)

This unit tells you when and why many religious poets re-told earlier Sanskrit works in their regional Indian languages.

Many religious poets in different parts of India composed poetry in regional languages to bring the teachings of earlier Sanskrit works from the Upanishads, the Bhagavata Purana and the Bhagavad-Gita within the reach of ordinary men and women. Jnanadeva lived in Maharashtra and wrote a long **Marathi** poem of 9000 verses in 1290CE, to explain the teachings of the Bhagavad-Gita. In the 16th century, Eknath wrote his Bhagavata in Marathi in order to explain the Bhagavata Purana to ordinary people in their own language. Ramadasa lived in Maharashtra in the 17th century. His Marathi book, the Dasabodha, is influenced by the teachings of the Bhagavad-Gita.

The states of India.

Here are some of Jnanadeva's words:

'The soul is different from the body.

The body is affected by consequences of actions.

The plant of ignorance can be uprooted only by wisdom.

A man of action is like the sun, doing his duty selflessly.

Devotion to God ends all sin and social status becomes meaningless.

God accepts any humble offering from a true devotee.'

The popularity of the Rama story

Other religious writers based their works in regional languages on the original Rama story, which is in Sanskrit. Eknath and Ramadasa both wrote their versions in Marathi to promote the worship of God Rama among people who did not know Sanskrit. In the ninth century the poet Kamban wrote a version of the story in **Tamil**, a south Indian language. A **Gujarati** translation of the Ramayana is popular. The poet Krittivasa translated the Ramayana from Sanskrit into **Bengali**; it is a very popular book in Bengal.

Tulsidas (16th century) lived in Uttar Pradesh, in north India. He wrote his **Hindi** version, called Rama-Charita-Manasa (The Lake of Rama's Deeds), in order to bring the teachings of earlier Sanskrit works to ordinary people. In the opening verse he says:

'I have written these verses in the local language (Hindi) to tell the Rama story. I have included the teachings of the Puranas and the Vedas in it. I have written the story from the Sanskrit Ramayana by Valmiki.'

All these religious writers felt that Hindu scriptures written in Sanskrit were keeping ordinary people away from the religious tradition. Sanskrit was used for religious writings for many centuries and the orthodox priests were not prepared to accept the scriptures written in regional languages. In spite of such opposition, writers such as Jnanadeva and Tulsidas produced their works in languages which people could understand. These writings in Hindi, Marathi, Bengali, Gujarati and Tamil are still popular today and continue the earlier religious tradition. For that reason they have the same authority as the Sanskrit scriptures in Hinduism.

NEW WORDS

Bengali, Gujarati, Hindi, Marathi, Tamil some of the fifteen official Indian languages

Jnanadeva
Jnanadeva (1275–96) was the foremost Maharashtrian saint and founder of the Marathi language and literature. His most famous work is a Marathi paraphrase of the Bhagavad-Gita called the Jnanesvari.
'Let the Lord of the Universe be pleased with this sacred literary activity of mine, and being pleased, let Him bestow on me this grace: May the wicked leave their crookedness and cultivate increasing love for the good. Let universal friendship reign among all beings. Let the darkness of evil disappear. Let the sun of true religion rise in the world. Let all beings obtain their desire. May all beings be endowed with all happiness and offer ceaseless devotion to the Primeval Being.'
(from Jnanesvari, 17.1794–1802)

This unit tells you how scriptures in regional languages promoted devotion to God. It also describes how manuscripts were prepared.

Hindu poets

Some religious poets who wrote in regional languages not only included the teachings of earlier Sanskrit scripture in their poetry but also promoted **Bhakti**, the devotional way of worshipping God. The practice of Bhakti requires a strong belief in a personal god of love and mercy. The worshipper delights in praising God, remembers God at all times and offers his or her life to the will of God.

Tukaram, a poet living in Maharashtra in the 17th century CE, wrote over 4000 hymns in Marathi stressing complete surrender to and limitless love for God. Here is one of his hymns. Vithoba and Keshava are names for Vishnu.

'May my speech repeat the sweet name of Vithoba.

May my eyes gaze joyfully on his divine face.

May my ears hear of his divine qualities.

Fly, O mind, and rest at the feet of Vithoba.

Hark, O soul, says Tuka, do not forsake Keshava'

Namadeva (14th century CE) wrote many songs in Marathi and stressed that social status was no barrier to following the way of Bhakti towards God.

Surdas (16th century CE) was a blind poet who lived at Agra, in north India. His Hindi verses describe Radha's devotion to God Krishna.

Mirabai (late 15th century CE) wrote devotional songs in Hindi, Braj Bhasha (a form of Hindi) and Gujarati. She was a princess and her devotion to God Krishna is seen in her many songs.

Here is one of them:

'You are my only refuge, O Krishna, the supporter of Mount Govardhana. Your crown of peacock feathers and your saffron-coloured garments are beautiful; your earrings have a unique splendour. Princess Draupadi stands helpless in full assembly. Protect her honour, O Murari. Mira's Lord Giridhara is indeed clever; his lotus-like feet are worthy of worship.'

The poet Kabir was a weaver by trade. He lived in the 15th century CE near Banaras. Orthodox priests persecuted him because he challenged their authority. He wrote devotional songs in Hindi, and maintained that Vishnu, Rama, Krishna and Allah were all names of the One Supreme God, who was neither in mosque nor in images. He preached devotion to God as a way of finding spiritual freedom.

Manuscripts

The Indian climate easily damages manuscript material. Animal skin (parchment) was considered 'impure' material for sacred writings, so in north India birch bark and birch leaves were used for recording sacred texts, and in the south, palm leaves were used. Paper was introduced into India in about 800CE but it was not used for sacred manuscripts until 1290CE.

Before the texts were written down on birch, the inner bark of the birch was cut into smooth pieces, which were fastened together with a cord. Reed pens and black ink were used for writing.

If palm was being used, the leaves were boiled, dried and flattened. A small hole was cut in each leaf so that the leaves could be held together in layers with a cord threaded through the holes. A pointed iron pencil was used to scratch the letters on palm leaves and soot or lamp-black was rubbed into the grooves.

The use of printing for sacred texts began in 1849CE. The Rig-Veda was printed in Sanskrit between 1849 and 1874. The Manava Kalpa Sutra in Sanskrit was printed in London in 1861. In the same year Kamban's Ramayana in Tamil was printed in

This palm leaf manuscript shows some verses from the Bhagavata Purana. This text stresses the importance of Bhakti, devotion to God.

Madras, India. Now sacred texts in all major Indian languages and scripts are available in printed books.

NEW WORD

Bhakti a way of worshipping a god or goddess by complete surrender to his or her will

Surdas
Surdas (16th century) was the blind poet-singer of Agra.

'I have danced my full now, O Gopal (Krishna)! With passion and fury as my petticoat, with lust for physical pleasure as my necklace, with delusion jingling as my anklets, with words of abuse as poetry, with mind full of false ideas as the big drum, with my movement in the company of the unholy as the steps, with avarice as the earthen pitcher making sound inside, beating time in various ways, I have danced enough. I have worn illusion as my girdle, I have put on material craving as the mark on my forehead; O do remove all this nonsense of mine!'

21 Law books

This unit is about the scriptures known as law books, which give the social and religious duties of the four traditional social groups in Hindu society.

Hindu law

All people have certain duties, depending on the job they do. Some duties are imposed by law, while others are optional, although there is a moral force behind them. For example, a nurse has a duty to provide medical care for the patient. A doctor has a duty to prescribe the correct treatment for the illness, yet the treatment must not be illegal. A lorry driver has a duty to obey all the traffic laws and to maintain the lorry in good condition, and must not carry any illegal goods. Nowadays, these laws are laid down by a body such as Parliament and people must follow them.

A long time ago, in traditional Hindu society, the duties of the four varnas (social groups) were laid down in scriptures called the Dharmashastra, ancient law books written in Sanskrit and recommending the religious and social duties of the people. These codes of behaviour had the force of law at first.

A bridegroom holds his bride's hand as she is given in marriage by her father.

Although they were based on laws believed to come from God, they were modified as time went on to suit the changing needs of society.

The code of Manu has 2685 verses and probably dates from 300CE. Manu says that right and wrong can be decided through the Vedas, traditional practice, good conduct of the righteous and a person's conscience.
The code of Yajnavalkya probably dates from 500CE. It, too, deals with dharma (religious and social duty) but stresses the legal aspect of social duties. These two codes largely formed the basis of Hindu law.

Hindu law is a personal law and applies to Hindus. It relates to adoption, marriage and divorce, and joint family properties. The laws passed by the Indian Parliament have reduced the importance of the ancient law books. Some rules from them are still useful, mainly those dealing with marriage and varna duties.

Here are some rules from the ancient law books:

Giving a girl in marriage

'A father, a grandfather, a brother or a male from the same family can give away a bride. If the seniormost male dies then the younger one in order can perform the ritual, provided he is of sound mind.'   (Yajnavalkya 1.63.)

Duties of Kshatriyas, Vaishyas and Shudras

'A Kshatriya's first duty is to protect people and property. Agriculture, banking, commerce and dairy-farming are suitable occupations for a Vaishya. Serving the three twice-born varnas is the duty of a Shudra. If a Shudra cannot get a good living by service, he may become a tradesman or learn a craft, but he should always serve the upper varnas.'
(Yajnavalkya 1.119–21.)

Importance of varna in marriage

'For the first marriage a bride from the same varna is recommended.'   (Manu 3.12.)

Duties of a Brahmin householder

'A Brahmin should earn a living and maintain his family by an occupation which does not affect other men's interest.

'A Brahmin's speech and feelings must befit his birth, wealth, age and education.

'No guest should be allowed to stay in a Brahmin's house without receiving hospitality, food, water and bed.

'He must not restrain a cow from drinking water or suckling her calf, if he sees her in those acts.'   (Manu 4.2, 18, 29, 59.)

Status of Women

'Women must be honoured and given clothes and ornaments by their fathers, brothers, husbands and brothers-in-law to promote (their own) good fortune.

'Where women are honoured, there the Gods shower blessings; but where they are ill treated, sacred rites bring no rewards.'
(Manu: 5.55–56.)

Evil and wicked actions
'Abusing (others), (speaking) untruth, detracting from the merits of all men, and talking idly, shall be the four kinds of (evil) verbal action.'
'Taking what has not been given, injuring (creatures) without the sanction of the law, and holding criminal intercourse with another man's wife, are declared to be three kinds of (wicked) bodily action.'
(The laws of Manu: 12. 6–7)

22 Hindu funerals

This unit shows how the Sutra texts describe the detailed performance of rituals, for example funerals.

We have already seen that the naming ceremony, the sacred thread ritual and weddings are carried out according to customs laid down in special books. It will not be too surprising to find that the way a funeral should be conducted is also set out in the Grihya Sutra of Ashwalayana.

Cremation

Cremation is the normal practice at Hindu funerals, but very young babies and **Sannyasins** (those who have given up all worldly ties) are buried. An ancient text gives a detailed description of a Hindu cremation:

'The corpse should be bathed by men if it is male, by women if it is female, and it should be dressed in new clothes. It is placed on a stretcher made of bamboo and carried to the cremation ground near a local river. The nearest male relative walks in front carrying some live coals in an earthenware pot. Slow-burning logs are used to build the pyre. Those who can afford it add a few sticks of sandalwood. The body is placed on the pyre with its head pointing to the north. The eldest or the youngest son of the deceased walks three times round the pyre with a lighted torch, then ignites the pyre at the four corners. When the pyre is burning strongly, he puts five spoonfuls of ghee onto the pyre as offerings to Agni, **Soma**, this world, Earth and the other world. The funerary priest chants mantras as the offerings of ghee are made. When the skull cracks through the action of heat, the atman is believed to escape into the atmosphere. Walking round the pyre with a lighted torch prevents the soul from escaping back to Earth and becoming a ghost to haunt the living.'

(Ashwalayana Grihya Sutra.)

A corpse is taken to the cremation ground.

A pyre is lighted to cremate the corpse.

The soul's destiny

Hindus believe that atman, the soul, never dies, but continues to exist in different bodies in successive lives. The body in the next life is determined by the consequences of actions in an earlier life.

Here is a verse from the oldest scripture, the Rig-Veda, addressed to the corpse as the funeral pyre is ignited:

> 'May your sight be absorbed into the sun and your atman escape into the atmosphere. May your atman reach the region of light or once more return to Earth, or perhaps go to the waters or to the plants, taking on new bodies, depending on the consequences of its actions.' (Rig-Veda 10.16.3.)

At the end of its long cycle of rebirths, the soul achieves its spiritual freedom and reaches Brahman.

NEW WORDS

Sannyasin a man who has given up all possessions and worldly ties to devote his life to God

Soma a sacred plant formerly used in Vedic ritual but now extinct

A Hindu funeral in Britain

In Britain a Hindu corpse is placed in a coffin and cremated. Religious rituals, such as walking round the corpse, are carried out at the funeral parlour. An incense stick is used instead of a lighted torch and, to console the mourners, verses from the Bhagavad-Gita are read in the chapel at the crematorium.

Verses addressed to the corpse
'The sages through penance won and increased their religious merit. May you go to them according to your penance.'
'Go to those who excelled in their penance and have achieved firm places in heaven, if your penance merits it.'
'Perhaps you will go to be among those who fought in battles and sacrificed their lives, or those who gave thousands of sacrificial gifts.'
'May this Earth be a pleasant, thornless resting place for this (departing) soul and give him a happy refuge.'
(Atharva-Veda: 18.2. 15–17, 19)

Index

The numbers in bold tell where the main definitions of the words are.